T0355593

ENGLISH HERITAGE

Hadrian's Wall Poster Pack

INFORMATION FOR TEACHERS

Hadrian's Wall and the Military Way crossing the River North Tyne.

ABOUT THIS POSTER PACK

This poster pack will help teachers explain to pupils how Hadrian's Wall was built, how it might have looked and how it functioned. It has been written and designed specifically for use by a whole class, working in groups, and will be useful for preparing pupils for a visit to Hadrian's Wall.

The pack contains aerial views and artists' impressions. There are eight A3 posters, with coloured images on one side and black and white images on the other. The latter can be photocopied to give you a total of sixteen invaluable visual sources for use in the classroom or to support on-site work. The accompanying notes give information about each poster and suggest ways that you can use them with pupils. They also assist the development of pupils' historical skills, including that of interpreting evidence from aerial photographs.

THE HISTORY OF THE WALL

Prior to the Wall the northern frontier of the Roman province of Britannia was a patrolled road, known as the Stanegate. It stretched from the Tyne to the Solway, linking a series of forts and watchtowers. When Hadrian arrived in Britain in AD 122 he decided to replace the Stanegate with a more physical barrier to control the frontier, perhaps as a consequence of recent unrest amongst British tribes. This barrier was to be a continuous wall stretching from Newcastle to Bowness on Solway with milecastles every Roman mile, two turrets in between and a ditch in front. The Wall was to be 3.5-4m high, and 76 miles long (about 111km), but was later extended by a further four Roman miles to the east to what is now Wallsend. It was built approximately 3km north of the Stanegate, across one of the narrowest parts of Britain. The garrison was to be

based in the forts along the Stanegate, with soldiers posted for periods of duty to the milecastles. However, shortly after construction work began on the Wall the plan was changed and it was decided to build a series of forts along its length, eventually numbering sixteen.

Hadrian was succeeded by Antoninus Pius who renewed attempts to conquer Scotland. He abandoned Hadrian's Wall, and within a short time reoccupied southern Scotland. A new frontier was established almost 100 miles further north between the Firth of Forth and the Firth of Clyde. This too was a wall, now known as the Antonine Wall, and was largely constructed of turf. However, by about AD 158 it was abandoned and Hadrian's Wall was reinstated as the frontier. A further attempt was made to conquer Scotland, but within a few years the army withdrew permanently to Hadrian's Wall.

The Wall was then continually occupied until periods of political instability in Rome and civil war within the empire resulted in large parts of the army being systematically recalled to Rome. Eventually in AD 410 the Emperor Honorius informed the province that it would have to defend itself. By then any remaining troops were recruited locally, operating more like a Home Guard rather than as a regular unit of the Roman army. Some of the forts continued to be inhabited, often by tribal chiefs and their families and livestock, but the Wall soon became a ready source of building stone for later homes, castles and farmsteads.

Constructing the Wall was a massive building task requiring the deployment of a huge number of men and the acquisition of vast amounts of materials.

HOW WAS THE WALL BUILT?

The Wall was constructed by work parties from three legions who built it in sections, approximately 8-10km long, at the same time. It was a huge undertaking that required vast amounts of different materials and a large labour force. Construction materials included enormous quantities of stone for building, along with limestone to make mortar. A substantial amount of clay was needed for the foundations of buildings, floor and roof tiles, and the core of the Wall itself. Timber was used as a building material, as well as being used for scaffolding, gates and roofs, fuel for the smiths and for burning lime. Iron was necessary for tools and hinges and lead was needed for water pipes. Most of these materials were available locally although some, such as iron and lead, were transported from other parts of Britain. Timber was readily available as the area was more heavily forested in Roman times.

The foundations of the entire length were laid out first, followed by the building of the turrets. They were constructed with masonry sticking out on either side so that they could be bonded to the Wall when it was eventually built.

The exterior of the Wall was built with square or rectangular blocks of sandstone. This was usually available locally, but in the central sector, the rock was too hard to be cut into blocks, and softer stone was brought from the east and west regions.

The core of the Wall was rubble, using any available stone, which was set in clay or mortar. When sections of the Wall needed rebuilding the rubble was set entirely in mortar. Roman mortar set very hard and was resistant to water and weather. It was produced from limestone, quarried near the Wall and burnt with charcoal in limekilns. This was then mixed with sand, gravel and water to produce mortar.

Originally the section from Birdoswald to the west coast was constructed of turf, but this was soon replaced with stone.

This poster contains two images. On one side is a drawing which has been adapted from a carving on Trajan's Column, erected in Rome in AD 113 to commemorate his campaigns in Dacia (Romania). It shows legionaries cutting logs and turf to construct a rampart. In the foreground soldiers are digging two ditches, while others are removing the earth in baskets or carrying turves on their shoulders. Some of the turves are held in place by short lengths of rope. The legionaries still wear their armour and carry their swords, but their javelins, helmets and shields are nearby (at the right of the drawing).

On the other side is an artist's impression which shows how legionary soldiers might have constructed a stretch of Hadrian's Wall. It is based on research and archaeological evidence, and shows men carrying out a variety of building tasks. In the foreground a centurion is supervising his men; in the middle ground a commander is surveying the work and in the distance is one of the stone turrets, which were built prior to the Wall. In this image the legionaries are not wearing armour.

Teaching activity

Use these two images to help pupils understand how the Wall was constructed and the efforts behind this massive building project.

Begin by showing pupils both images and asking them to look for differences and similarities. When pupils notice that the legionaries are wearing armour in only one of the images, ask them to suggest why. (It is probable that in the black and white drawing the legionaries are building a marching camp in hostile territory whereas in the colour image the soldiers are building the Wall in an area, which has already been subdued.)

Then ask pupils to list:
■ what materials are being used
■ where the materials might have come from
■ what tools are being used
■ what jobs are being done.

Finally ask pupils to suggest all the different skills that were needed to carry out this huge building task.

At every Roman mile were milecastles, and between each pair were two turrets. They acted as look out positions and signalling points.

HOW WAS THE WALL DEFENDED?

Many artists' impressions show the Wall with a wall-walk and parapet, but there is no conclusive proof that these existed. Even without them, the Wall could be defended by the milecastles that were built every Roman mile (1.6km) along its length and the two intervening turrets. Also, to the north of the Wall there was a ditch, usually 8-12m wide and 2.7-3m deep, to deter attackers charging at the Wall.

The milecastles provided temporary living accommodation for soldiers patrolling the Wall. They were built to a standard square plan with one or two long buildings of either timber or stone, which usually accommodated up to 32 men. They had two gateways: one in their south wall and another through the Wall itself. Milecastles also operated as fortified crossing points, enabling the army to control the movement of people across the frontier as well as to levy taxes on goods passing through.

The turrets were not built as living quarters or passage points through the Wall, and are therefore quite basic. In the centre of the floor was a hearth used for keeping warm and cooking. Access to the upper floor and walkway was by a ladder. Each was sited to be visible to its neighbouring turret or milecastle to provide mutual security and to assist lines of communication. This image is only one possible interpretation of how a turret may have looked.

Later additions to the Wall were the vallum and the Military Way, built on its south side. The vallum was a flat-bottomed ditch with a bank on either side, intended to protect the garrison from being attacked from behind. In some places it runs very close to the Wall, but in others it is up to 1km away. Crossing points were built to provide access to the forts. The Military Way runs parallel to the Wall and links all the forts.

This poster has line drawings of a milecastle and turret and a colour aerial photograph that shows the course of the vallum cutting through the landscape. Also on this aerial photograph are the rectangular outlines of a series of practice camps, dug as part of the soldiers' routine training and drill.

Teaching activities

Use this poster to help pupils understand how the frontier was defended, its different components and what soldiers did when they were on duty.

Give pupils photocopies of the milecastle and turret and ask them to identify all the defensive elements of the two structures. Get them to label each one, explaining what each was intended to do and how they functioned. Look at the aerial view that shows the vallum. How much did the Roman legionary builders use the landscape as part of their defensive planning? What were the defensive elements of the vallum, and how effective do pupils think they were?

Then you could ask pupils to imagine themselves as a commanding officer in charge of a stretch of Wall and vallum, a milecastle and the two turrets on either side of it. Assign pupils a specific number of soldiers under their command, perhaps sixteen, then tell them to work out:

■ how they would organise a duty roster over 24 hours
■ how they would deploy their men on guard duty
■ what other routine tasks would need to be done
■ what equipment they would need
■ what orders they would give if under attack or if a hostile group approached.

WHAT DID THE FORTS LOOK LIKE?

The forts along the Wall usually had a common plan - rectangular with rounded corners - and were surrounded by at least one ditch. All had a high surrounding stone wall with towers at regular intervals and a double gateway on each side. Most had three gateways opening north of the Wall, especially cavalry forts, so that the army could advance quickly towards an approaching enemy.

Behind the fort wall was an earth rampart into which bakehouses and ovens were built, separated from other buildings owing to the risk of fire.

Most of the forts along the line of Hadrian's Wall followed a standard plan with the central part containing the most important buildings.

Inside, the fort was divided into three areas with the most important buildings (headquarters building, the commanding officer's house, the granaries and often a hospital) in the centre. On either side were the barracks, stables and workshops. A bathhouse was usually situated outside, owing to the risk of fire.

Around the south side of the forts a civilian settlement (vicus) quickly developed. At first the buildings were simple timber structures, but as the settlement developed many were rebuilt in stone. Their inhabitants had recognised the potential spending power of a large military presence and set up businesses to trade with them and to provide for their needs. These included inns, shops and lodging houses. There were also temples, as many soldiers originated from other parts of the Empire and still worshipped their gods from home, but usually only the official Roman gods could be worshipped in the forts. Workshops were also built outside forts as many would pose a fire risk if sited within. Eventually, when soldiers were allowed to have families and the size of the garrison was reduced they may have moved their families into the fort.

This poster features two different artists' impressions of Housesteads Fort, and an aerial view of the surviving remains. Both the impressions are based on the same evidence and demonstrate the plan of a fort, its rigid road pattern, the uniformity of some of the buildings and how they might have looked.

Teaching activities
Use this poster to help pupils understand the layout of a fort and how artist's impressions can be produced, based on physical and archaeological evidence. You can also use this poster to demonstrate how pupils' impressions of life inside a fort can be influenced by the style of the artist. Below are two suggestions.

Look at the aerial view first and ask pupils what they can detect about the organisation of a fort. Also, how

The headquarters building occupied a central position of the fort, and was the operations centre.

does the fort relate to the Wall? Then show pupils one or both of the artists' impressions. What else do these images tell them about a fort? Look at the size, shape and design of the buildings. Ask why there are so many long buildings at each side and why the buildings in the middle might be different. Why is the settlement (vicus) situated where it is? Point out that this fort was built to house almost 1000 men, though not all were billeted there at the same time. What might it have been like inside?

Divide your group into two, giving each only one artist's impression of the fort and a large sheet of white paper. Tell pupils that they are looking at an artist's impression of how the fort may have looked, and you want them to make a list of words or short phrases that convey what it might have been like to live and serve there. Then without revealing either of the pictures place the lists side by side and compare them. After discussion, reveal both images and ask pupils which image they think really shows what the fort was like, and why. Can they agree? Finally, sum up by asking them what they think was the purpose of this exercise (that artists' impressions can differ and can give a biased view of what a site may have been like).

HOW WERE THE FORTS COMMANDED?
The two main buildings connected with the running of the fort were the headquarters building and the commanding officer's house.

The headquarters building was the operations centre of the fort, and occupied a central position. It was divided into three sections: an open courtyard surrounded by a colonnade on three sides; an assembly hall; and a row of five small rooms. The courtyard was a meeting place and often contained a well. The assembly hall was used for business, hearings and ceremonies; at one end was a platform on which the commanding officer would address his officers. Large double doors ensured that the hall could be evacuated in an emergency. The row of small rooms were offices, with a shrine in the middle which housed the regimental standards, a statue to the emperor and altars to official gods. As the shrine was the most sacred part of the fort it was always guarded and was therefore an ideal place to build an underground strongroom to hold the army's pay and pension. This is clearly seen at Chesters and at Corbridge, but at Housesteads the underlying rock was too hard to construct an underground room.

The soldiers lived in rows of closely-built barracks, with units of eight men sharing one room.

The commanding officer's house was the largest and most luxurious building in the fort. It housed not only himself and his family, but also an extensive personal staff. The commanding officer was a senior figure in Roman administration and he expected a home that reflected his status. He would often entertain passing important dignitaries. The house was built in the style of town houses in Rome, with rooms around four sides of a large central courtyard. Many of his personal rooms would have had underfloor heating and decorated plastered walls. He would also have had a private bath suite, such as the one that can be seen at Chesters. Other rooms in his house included kitchens, stables and servants' accommodation.

On one side of this poster are artist's impressions of the commanding officer's house and the headquarters building at Housesteads. On the reverse are drawings showing how their interiors might have looked.

Teaching activities

Use this poster to examine the lifestyle of a military commander, and the business of running a fort.

Commanding officer's house.

Ask pupils what the exterior picture tells them about his status and his expectations of life in the fort. Pose questions such as why did his house need to be so big? What would all the rooms have been used for? How would he have used the enclosed courtyard? What materials were used to build his house? Then look at the cutaway image and identify how different rooms were used. Which were the most important and how can they tell? Why might the slaves' rooms be situated where they were? Which part was the least decorated and why? Look for the doorways to see where they led. Why did some rooms not open onto the courtyard, but could only be entered from other rooms?

Headquarters building. Ask

pupils why a fort would need such a building. What functions do they think would be carried out in it? Then look at the cut-away image to decide where these would be carried out. Give reasons for their decisions. Why was the shrine placed in the middle of the row of offices and directly opposite the main entrance? (To provide a focal point that was immediately opposite the main entrance.)

Then, in anticipation of a visit to a site along the Wall, ask pupils to consider what they might expect to see of either building after it had been abandoned for sixteen hundred years. What materials might have decayed, been stolen or reused for other buildings?

WHAT WAS DAILY LIFE LIKE FOR A SOLDIER?

While the commanding officer and his household lived in a large, luxurious house and the centurions lived in spacious accommodation with their servants at the end of each barrack block, the average infantry soldier lived in long, closely-built barrack blocks, sharing his living space with seven other men. He stored his equipment in a small room at the front and slept with his unit in the room to the rear. A cavalry soldier, however, shared his space with only two other men, using the front part of his barrack to stable his horse, and storing his equipment in his sleeping space.

Each soldier made his bread by grinding his daily corn ration on shared querns (handmill), then baking the mixture in communal ovens around the edge of the fort. Even cooking his food was a group activity, using the hearth inside his barrack room. Often, soldiers took advantage of the bars, shops and eating places in the settlement (vicus) outside the forts, perhaps eating with families or girlfriends.

Not only was a soldier required to work, sleep and prepare his food with his comrades, he had to bathe and visit the latrines in their company too. However, attitudes were different then, and it was not seen as an inconvenience. In fact bathing was regarded as a social event. The bathhouse was situated outside the fort with a series of cold, warm and hot rooms, with plunge baths. Here, apart from bathing, men could socialise, exercise, gamble, eat and drink or relax. This afforded some relief from the often basic, cold and cramped conditions inside the barracks.

For the average soldier, using the latrines was also a communal affair. The latrine block at Housesteads could accommodate several men, and it is believed there were no partitions between the seats and no roof to the building. The only protection for the sitter was a canopy, and even that had an additional function - to direct rainwater into a central channel that fed water below the seats to help flush the waste away.

This poster shows the different buildings that the troops would have used on a daily basis. It contains artists' impressions of the infantry barracks at Housesteads, the cavalry barracks at Chesters, the latrines at Housesteads and the bathhouse at Chesters.

Teaching activities
Use this poster to consider the living and working conditions of the soldiers in the forts.

Compare the images of the two barrack blocks. List any similarities and differences. Ask pupils to look at building materials, the roadway in between, and drainage. How might each row of barracks look in different weather conditions, or in the evening when most soldiers have returned from their different duties?

The image of Chesters does not show horses, as it was drawn at the time when there was no clear evidence of where they were stabled. However, recent excavations at Wallsend Fort suggest that horses were stabled in the front room of barrack blocks. Given this information, how might this alter the artist's impression at Chesters? What other sights, sounds and smells might accompany this image?

Discuss differences in the way we take a bath today and visit the toilet. Remember that the Romans considered themselves to be very civilised, and were very proud of their achievements in public sanitation. Given that the barracks had no private bathing or toilet facilities, how would this affect the daily life and routine of a soldier in the fort?

Camps and civilian settlements soon grew up around forts catering for the recreational needs of the soldiers.

Large towns like Corbridge would have brought a wide variety of people together from across the Empire.

WHAT DID SOLDIERS DO WHEN ON LEAVE?

On a day-to-day basis soldiers would have had the option of staying in their barracks or going into the settlement (vicus) immediately outside the fort, even if only to escape the rigours of military discipline and the cramped living conditions. Many did so because there was recreation in the form of inns and taverns where they could eat, drink, talk and gamble. There were even brothels, though it was quite common for soldiers, who were not legally allowed to marry, to have wives or girlfriends, sometimes with children, living in the vicus. Officers were able to go hunting, and hunt cups, mementos or trophies of their hunts, can be seen in museums such as Corbridge and Chesters.

For longer periods of leave soldiers may have visited nearby towns such as Corbridge to escape the rigours of military routine. Here they would find markets and shops selling a variety of luxury items that were not available in the settlements outside the forts, and which had been brought by merchants from other regions of Britain or the Empire. There would also be the opportunity to meet comrades serving at different parts of the Wall.

This poster shows an artist's impression of the settlement outside Housesteads Fort, perhaps typical of that outside many forts, and an artist's impression of the much larger town of Corbridge.

Teaching activities

Use this poster to look at how soldiers spent their time when off duty. Photocopy the black and white image and ask pupils to compare it with the aerial view of Corbridge. What activities can pupils see happening? Look for different types of buildings and list how they might have been used. Which ones would a soldier likely visit?

Discuss why a soldier might want to go to the settlement outside the fort. What would he do there? Why might a soldier want to go to Corbridge town? What would he do there that he could not do at the settlement outside his fort? How might he feel about returning to his fort?

As an extension you could ask pupils to compare the styles of the two artists. How does this influence their view about life along the frontier in Roman times? Alternatively, you could look at how the buildings are different. Look at their shape, style and construction materials. Why should there be any differences? How are the two settlements planned?

WHO LIVED AND WORKED ALONG THE FRONTIER?

The large concentration of people living along the frontier would have been a very diverse mix. Many came from other countries, including soldiers recruited from other provinces of the Empire and merchants who had travelled to the frontier to take advantage of trading opportunities with such a large military force. The population would also have come from many social classes, with different military ranks such as the fort commander, senior officers, centurions and auxiliary troops, and civilians that included Roman citizens, local Britons, merchants, craftsmen and slaves. Many of these people would come together, intentionally or otherwise, in major towns such as Corbridge.

This poster shows two busy street scenes from Corbridge town where a variety of people are engaged in a range of activities.

Teaching activities

Use this poster to highlight the social and ethnic mix of Roman society.

Begin by asking pupils to identify different groups of people. Who might be local people and who might be visitors? Who is rich and who is not? Who are the most important people? How can they tell? Pick out which people are working and who are not. List the jobs they are doing and the objects they are using. Look for pairs or groups of people engaged in conversation. Photocopy either poster and ask pupils to make speech bubbles to convey what they might be discussing. Or, use thought bubbles to suggest what individuals might be thinking at that moment. What is their view or opinion of other people in the scene?

Many more approaches for using this poster, and others in this pack, can be found in Interpreting the Past poster pack, see Useful Resources on page 8.

Aerial view of how Roman Corbridge may have looked.

HOW LARGE WERE THE SETTLEMENTS?

Most of the sites along Hadrian's Wall frontier have not been fully excavated and many buildings still lie beneath the soil. However, it is not always necessary to excavate to determine the presence and shape of buried features. Other means of discovery include using aerial photographs. Taken early morning or late afternoon when the sun is lower, the contours of surface features are more sharply revealed by their shadows. Crop marks, too can reveal information, especially buried remains. They are particularly prominent in times of drought when crops growing above buried features do not grow as tall, and their hollows create shadows of the contours of buried features. (This can also be seen on the aerial photograph of the vallum and practice camps.) Infrared photography is another means of locating buried features.

This poster contains an aerial photograph image of Corbridge town taken with an infra-red camera, showing evidence of many other buildings and roadways that have not been excavated. The two plans on the back are of the excavated section and of the wider settlement based on the evidence of the aerial photograph.

Teaching activities

Use this poster to help pupils identify the clues that enabled archaeologists to work out how large the site may have been. This activity requires pupils to look closely, to analyse and to interpret evidence. This will then help them to make their own deductions about what it might have been like to have lived in the town.

Give pupils the plan of the whole site and the aerial photograph. First, ask them to identify the features that are visible above ground, then to look for those below ground that helped archaeologists show the extent of the town in Roman times. How many different shaped buildings can they see? What is the most common shape for buildings, and what might they have been used for? Look for larger buildings, and ask pupils to describe their shape and layout. Find the roads - main routes and lesser ones. What types of buildings are on either side of them? Discuss what this information tells them about the town of Corbridge and what it might have been like to have lived there.

Alternatively, place a plan of only the excavated features in the middle of a large piece of paper. Give pupils the aerial photograph and ask them to find evidence of buried features and mark this on their site plans. After a given period you can give pupils copies of the plan that was drawn by aerial archaeologists to compare.

USEFUL RESOURCES

Teacher handbooks
Walmsley, D, *Hadrian's Wall Teacher Handbook*, English Heritage, 2002, ISBN 1-85074 - 823-3.
Watson, I, *Using Roman Sites*, English Heritage, 1997, ISBN 1-85074-334-7.

Posters
Roman Britain, English Heritage, 1997, ISBN 1-85074-684-2. Contains eight A3 posters.
Interpreting the Past, English Heritage, 1999, ISBN 1-85074-737-7. Contains six colour posters with 8-page booklet with activities to help teachers use artists' impressions on site and in the classroom. Many of the teaching approaches can easily be used with the posters in this pack.
Time Detectives, English Heritage, 2002, ISBN 1-85074- 778-4. Contains six A3 posters with 8-page teacher booklet with curriculum ideas.
Real Romans, English Heritage, 2002, ISBN 1-85074-812-8. Contains six A3 posters.

Maps
Roman Britain, historical map and guide, Ordnance Survey, ISBN 0-319-29029-8.

Aerial photographs
Additional aerial photographs are available from the National Monuments Record Centre, Kemble Drive, Swindon, SN2 2GZ. Tel 01793 414600. E-mail: nmrinfo@english-heritage.org.uk

CD ROM
Real Romans, English Heritage/TAG, 1999, ISBN 1-902604-00-7. Includes 48-page book.

Videos
Talkin' Roman, English Heritage, 1996, 20 mins. Suitability: Key Stage 2. Investigates life in Britain under the Romans using characters from the past.
Hadrian's Wall - A journey back in time, 1998, 48 mins.

English Heritage is the national leader in heritage education. It aims to help teachers at all levels to use the historic environment. Each year it welcomes over half a million pupils, students and teachers on free educational group visits to over 400 sites in its care. For copies of the Free Educational Visits booklets, the Resources catalogue, and Heritage Learning, our termly magazine, contact:
English Heritage Education
Freepost 22 (WD214)
London W1E 7EZ
Tel. 020-7973 3442
Fax. 020-7973 3443
www.HeritageEducation.net

Written and produced by David Walmsley
Designed by Alan McPherson
Illustrations by Alan Sorrell, Philip Corke, Ivan Lapper, Peter Dunn, Peter Connolly, David Hall and Frank Gardiner.
Aerial photographs © English Heritage
Printed by Hythe Offset
© English Heritage 2002

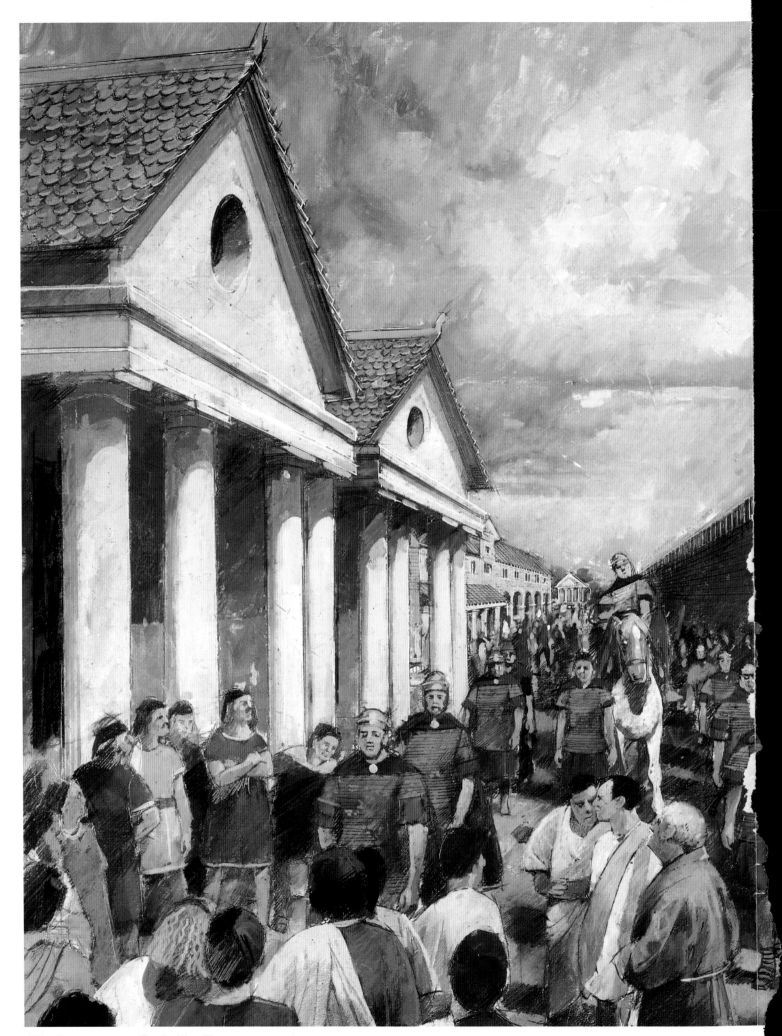

The Stanegate at Corbridge Town

Outside the Forum Building at Corbridge Town

WHAT WAS DAILY LIFE LIKE FOR A SOLDIER?

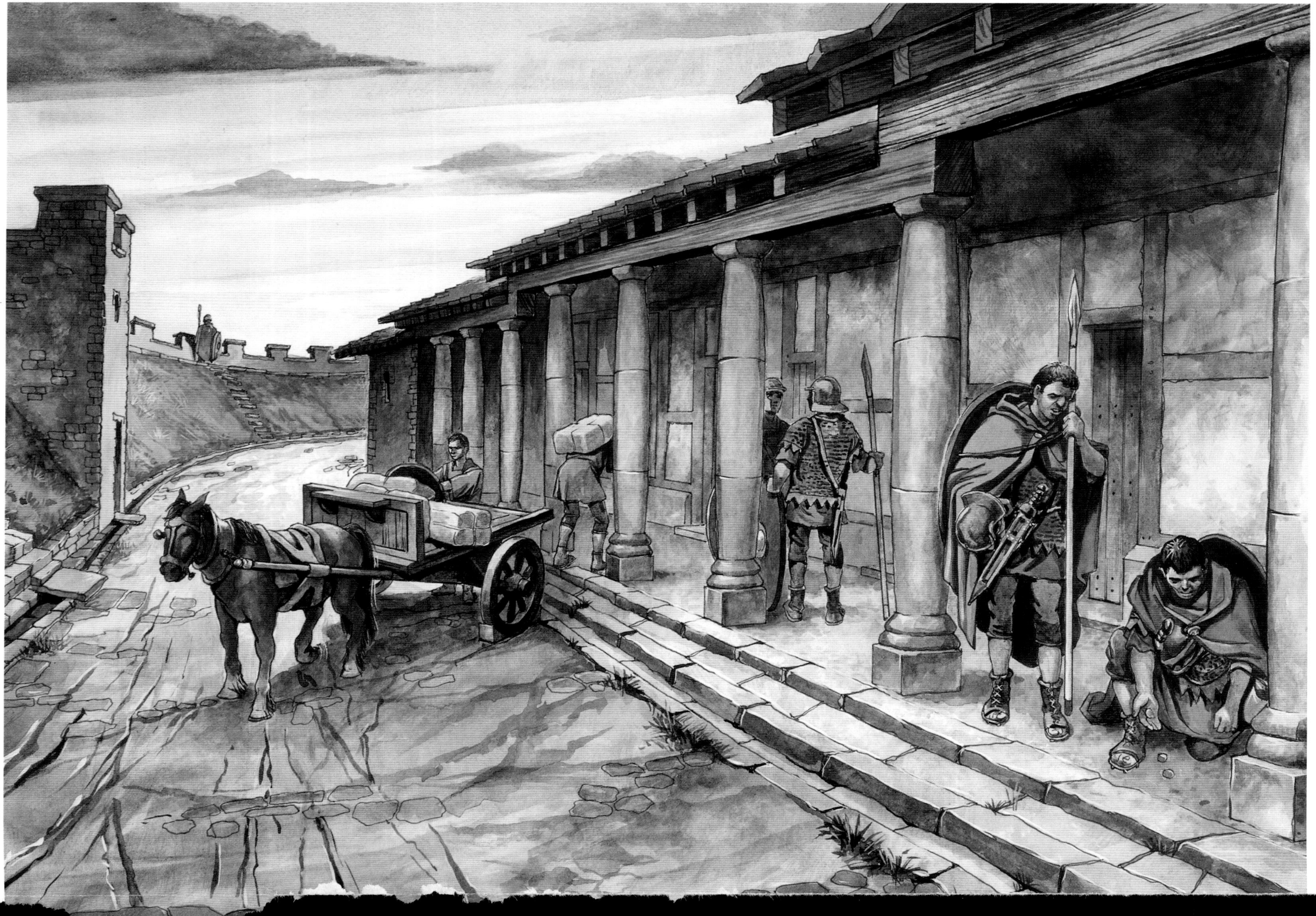

Infantry Barracks at Housesteads Fort

Cavalry Barracks at Chesters Fort

Housesteads Fort

Housesteads Fort

WHAT DID SOLDIERS DO WHEN ON LEAVE?

Corbridge Roman Town

The settlement outside Housesteads Fort

Richard Sorrell 1986

© English Heritage

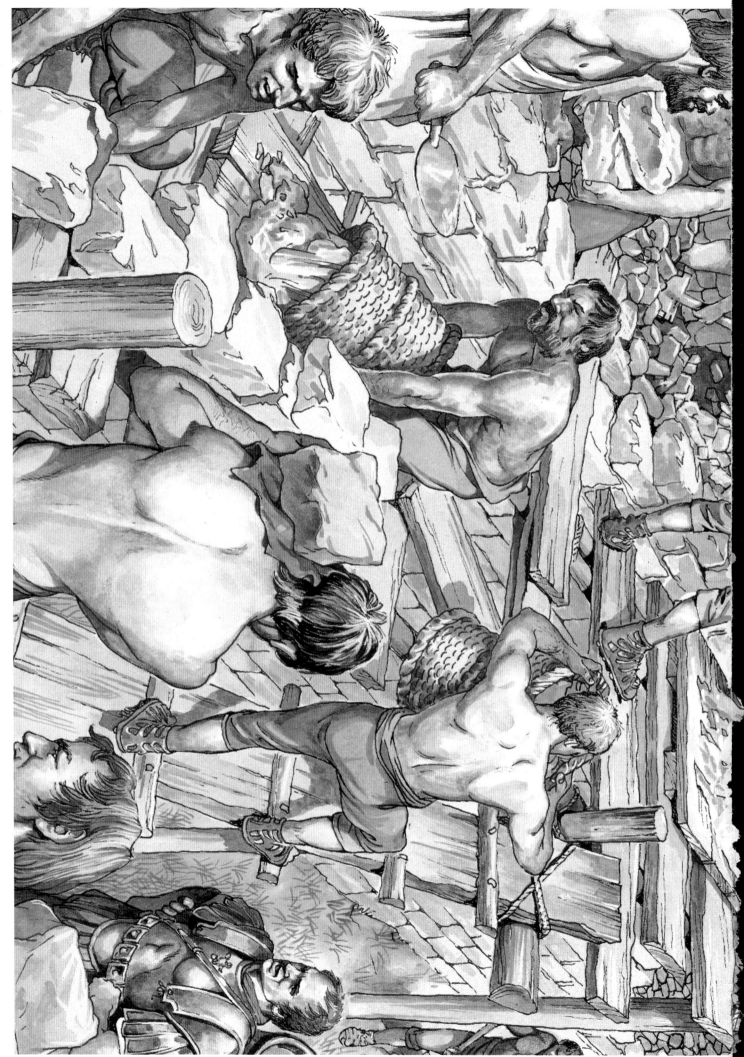

HOW WAS THE WALL BUILT?

Line drawing taken from Trajan's Column

HOW LARGE WERE THE SETTLEMENTS?

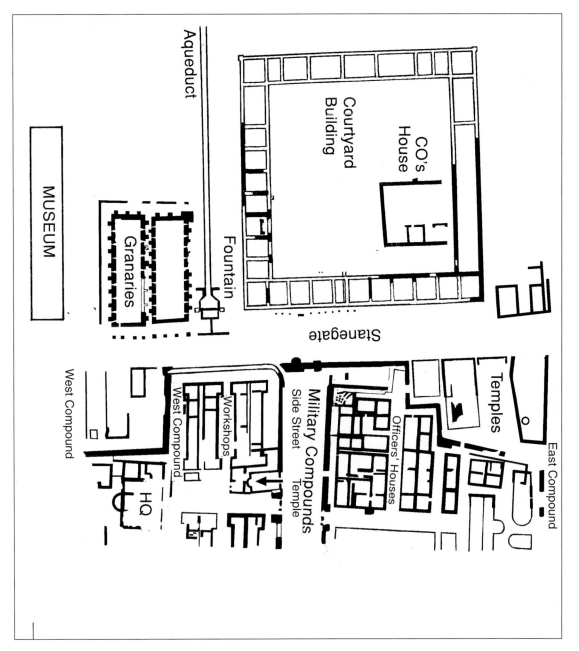

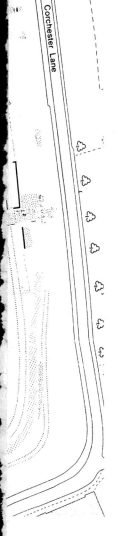

Plan of excavated remains at Corbridge Town

Infra-red aerial photograph of Corbridge Town

Plan of Corbridge Town based on aerial photographic evidence

Cor Burn

River Tyne

© English Heritage

Milecastle

HOW WAS THE WALL DEFENDED?

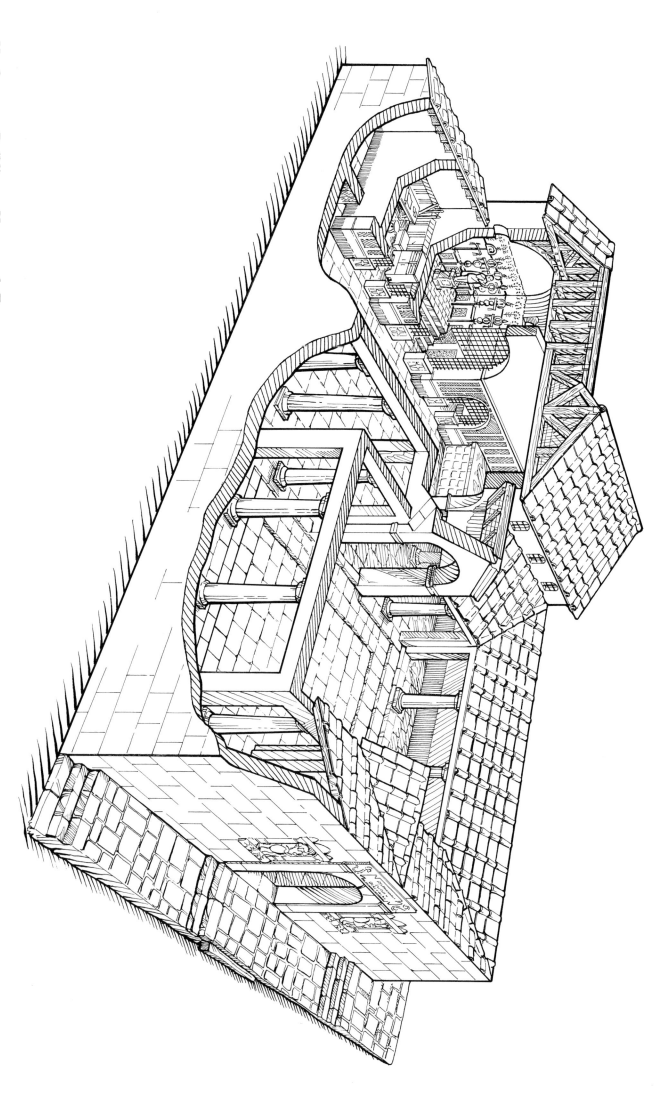

Headquarters Building at Housesteads Fort

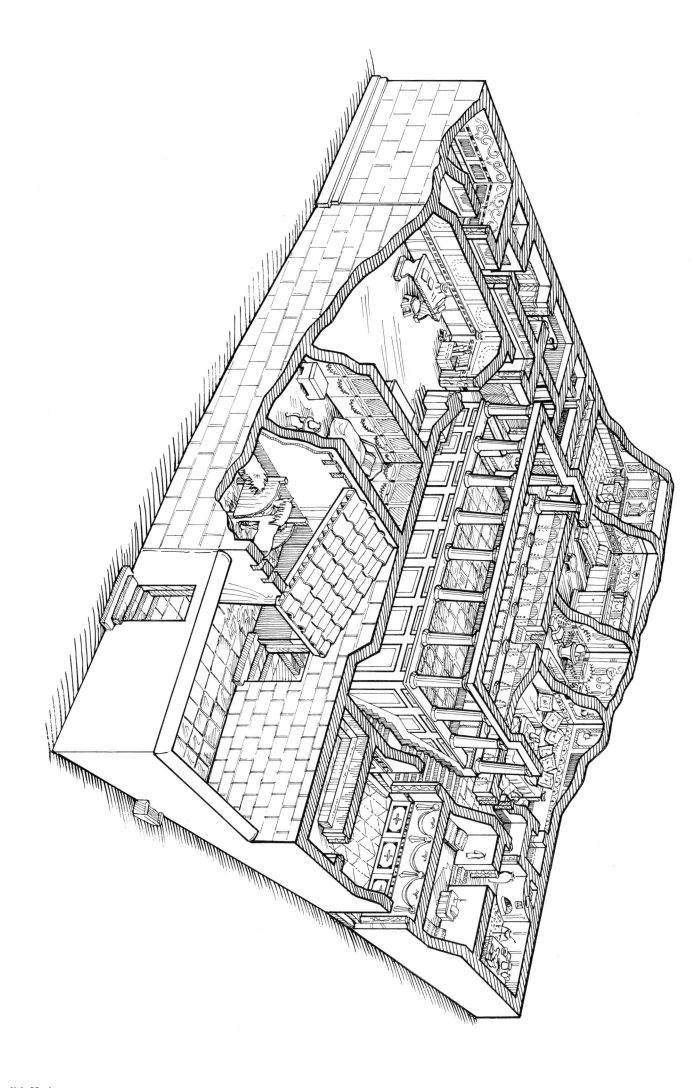